Legumes

WORLD'S BEST
✳
RECIPES

Alexandre Libedinsky

MACMILLAN CANADA
TORONTO

First published in English in Canada in 2000 by
Macmillan Canada, an imprint of CDG Books Canada

Canadian Cataloguing in Publication Data

Libedinsky, Alexandre, 1963 —
        World's best legume recipes

Translation of: Les légumineuses.
Includes index.
ISBN 0-7715-7717-6

1. Cookery (Legumes). I. Title.

TX803.B4L5213 2000   641.6'565   C00-932260-4

This book is available at special discounts for bulk purchases by your group or organization for sales promotions, premiums, fundraising and seminars. For details, contact: CDG Books Canada Inc., 99 Yorkville Avenue, Suite 400, Toronto, ON, M5R 3K5.

1 2 3 4 5 TOTAL 04 03 02 01 00

Design and layout.:	Cyclone Design Communications Inc.
Photography:	François Croteau
Project manager:	Gisèle LaRocque
Translation:	Katrin Sermat
Revision:	Mark Daly
Proofreading:	Jane Jackel
Indexing:	Diane Baril

Macmillan Canada
An imprint of CDG Books Canada Inc.
Toronto

Printed in Canada

Contents

Introduction

Easy and fast, the delicious recipes in this book are a great way to discover the many pleasures and possibilities of legumes.

Legumes, or pulses, have always had a place in the diet. Rich in protein and low in fat, legumes are growing in popularity today although they have long figured among the staple foods of many cultures.

You don't have to be a vegetarian to appreciate legumes. As you will see, this book contains recipes for a variety of legume-based dishes or side dishes that will add colour, flavour and originality to your table.

Hints

Although canned beans and peas are practical, you'll find a greater variety of dried legumes. One cup (250 mL) of dried legumes will yield 2 to 3 cups (500 mL to 750 mL) once cooked.

Contrary to popular belief, legumes do not have to be soaked before cooking. Just wash them well under cold water and, after picking out any broken ones, place them in a large pot covered with 3 to 4 times their volume in cold water. Be sure never to salt the water, since that toughens the skins of peas and beans. Bring to a boil, skim and simmer over very low heat for the recommended cooking time (see table). Once the legumes are done, rinse them under cold water and drain. They can be refrigerated for 48 hours or frozen for 6 months.

Cooked legumes freeze very well. Place them in a single layer on a tray, cover with plastic wrap and freeze for 12 hours. Remove the tray from the freezer; the legumes separate easily. Store them in the freezer in a hermetically sealed container or bag. When using, remove only the required quantity of legumes and thaw them in hot water.

Never cook legumes in the microwave oven, since they must be slow cooked to become tender. Use the microwave only to reheat dishes such as soups and casseroles. In addition, if using a pressure cooker, ensure that it is no more than half full of water and legumes, and divide the cooking times listed in the table by one half.

A tip for preventing flatulence: rinse legumes under cold water once cooked. If you eat them regularly, your system will adapt and you'll have fewer problems with gas.

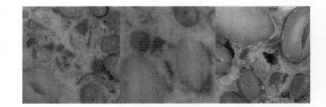

Cooking Times

Black beans	1 hour
Black-eyed peas	45 minutes
Chickpeas	1 1/2 to 2 hours
Fava beans	1 to 1 1/2 hours
Flageolets	1 hour
Green lentils	35 minutes
Green split peas	30 minutes
Lima beans	1 to 1 1/2 hours
Mixed beans	1 to 1 1/2 hours
Mung beans	40 minutes
Pigeon peas	1 to 1 1/2 hours
Pinto beans	1 hour
Puy lentils	35 minutes
Red beans	1 hour
Red kidney beans	1 to 1 1/2 hours
Romano beans	1 hour
White beans	1 hour
Yellow split peas	30 minutes

Soups, Sauces, Coulis

Soups, Sauces, Coulis

Cream of Kidney Beans with Cloves

Lentil Minestrone

Chickpea Soup with Spinach

Black Bean Coulis

Mustard Sauce with Green Lentils

White Beans with Pasta

Chicken Broth with Fava Beans and Pesto

Tropical Mixed Bean Salsa

Pico de Gallo with Lentils and Melons

Cajun Butter with Kidney Beans

Cream of Kidney Beans with Cloves

4 servings

INGREDIENTS

15 mL olive oil **1 tbsp**

1 medium-sized onion, finely chopped **1**

1 medium-sized garlic clove, chopped **1**

400 g cooked red kidney beans or one 540 mL (19-oz) can red kidney beans, rinsed and drained **2 cups**

1 potato, peeled and diced **1**

2 cloves, crushed **2**

Pinch ground white pepper

1 mL salt **1/4 tsp**

750 mL water or chicken stock **3 cups**

60 mL 35% cream **1/4 cup**

METHOD

1   In a large pot, sauté the onion and garlic over medium heat for 4 to 5 minutes. Add the beans, potato cubes, cloves and all other ingredients except the cream. Partially cover and bring to a boil. Skim off any foam that forms on the surface and simmer for 20 minutes.

2   Purée the soup in a blender or food processor and pass through a strainer.

3   Serve piping hot. Swirl in the 35% cream.

Lentil Minestrone

6 to 8 servings

INGREDIENTS

15 mL olive oil **1 tbsp**

250 mL diced onion **1 cup**

250 mL diced carrot **1 cup**

3 stalks celery, diced **3**

125 mL diced turnip **1/2 cup**

125 mL diced zucchini **1/2 cup**

125 mL diced red pepper **1/2 cup**

10 mL dried basil **2 tsp**

5 mL dried oregano **1 tsp**

2 mL dried thyme **1/2 tsp**

10 mL salt **2 tsp**

1 can 796 mL (28 oz) diced tomatoes drained **1**

2 L water or chicken stock **8 cups**

2 cloves garlic **2**

150 g frozen green peas, blanched **2/3 cup**

400 g cooked green lentils or one 540 mL (19-oz) can green lentils, rinsed and drained **2 cups**

METHOD

1 In a large pot, heat the olive oil over medium heat and sauté all the diced vegetables—except the tomatoes, peas and lentils—garlic and seasonings for 8 to 10 minutes. Allow the vegetables to caramelize slightly.

2 Add the tomatoes and water. Simmer for 20 minutes, partially covered.

3 Add the remaining ingredients and simmer, uncovered, for another 5 minutes. Serve hot, with garlic croutons.

Chickpea Soup with Spinach

6 to 8 servings

INGREDIENTS

15 mL olive oil **1 tbsp**

3 medium-sized onions, diced **3**

1 clove garlic **1**

2 mL ground cumin **1/2 tsp**

Pinch ground white pepper

10 mL salt **2 tsp**

Pinch cayenne pepper

2.5 L water or chicken stock **10 cups**

3 potatoes, diced (about 400 g) **3**

800 g cooked chickpeas or two 540 mL (19-oz) cans chickpeas, rinsed and drained **4 cups**

500 g fresh spinach, washed, stems removed and chopped **2 cups**

METHOD

1 In a large pot, heat the olive oil over medium heat, and cook the onions and garlic with the seasonings. Add the water and cook, covered, over low heat for 20 minutes.

2 Add the potatoes and cook until they are tender but still slightly crunchy.

3 Add the chickpeas and bring to a boil again; keep warm.

4 Garnish bowls with chopped spinach and serve the soup very hot. The spinach will cook in the hot soup.

Black Bean Coulis

4 to 6 portions

This coulis goes well with patés, grilled meat or fish.

INGREDIENTS

15 mL olive oil **1 tbsp**

1 mL ground caraway seeds **1/4 tsp**

1 mL dried coriander **1/4 tsp**

1 mL cardamom **1/4 tsp**

1 mL salt **1/4 tsp**

Pinch cayenne pepper

1 medium-sized onion, chopped **1**

1 clove garlic, minced **1**

400 g cooked black beans or one 540 mL (19-oz) can black beans, rinsed and drained **2 cups**

250 mL water **1 cup**

METHOD

1 In a pot, cook all the spices in oil over medium heat for about 3 to 4 minutes or until they become fragrant.

2 Add the onion, garlic and beans, and continue cooking for another 5 minutes. Add the water and bring to a boil. Skim off any foam and cook for another 2 minutes.

3 When done, cool for 10 minutes.

4 Purée in a blender or food processor (taking care not to get burned by the steam). Filter through a strainer.

Mustard Sauce with Green Lentils

4 to 6 servings

This sauce can be served hot or cold with poultry, pork or veal.

INGREDIENTS

15 mL olive oil **1 tbsp**

1 medium-sized onion, chopped **1**

1 clove garlic, chopped **1**

5 mL dried tarragon **1 tsp**

2 mL paprika **1/2 tsp**

Pinch white pepper

1 mL salt **1/4 tsp**

Pinch cayenne pepper

400 g cooked green lentils or one 540 mL (19-oz) can green lentils, rinsed and drained **2 cups**

250 mL water or chicken stock **1 cup**

125 mL 35% cream **1/2 cup**

5 mL Dijon mustard **1 tsp**

METHOD

1 In a 2 L (8-cup) pot, heat the olive oil over low heat and cook the onion, garlic and seasonings for about 5 minutes.

2 Add the lentils and cream and bring to a boil.

3 Skim off any foam and simmer for another 5 minutes. Remove from heat. Whisk in the mustard.

4 Purée in a blender or food processor and pour through a strainer.

White Beans with Pasta

4 to 6 servings

INGREDIENTS

250 g blanched smoked bacon, julienned 8 oz

1 large onion, chopped 1

1 clove garlic, chopped 1

2 carrots, chopped 2

5 mL dried oregano 1 tsp

2 mL dried basil 1/2 tsp

1 mL dried thyme 1/4 tsp

10 mL paprika 2 tsp

2 mL salt 1/2 tsp

1 bay leaf 1

Pinch cayenne pepper

10 mL tomato paste 2 tsp

2 L water or chicken stock 8 cups

400 g cooked white beans or one 540 mL (19-oz) can white beans, rinsed and drained 2 cups

300 g cooked linguine or spaghetti 11 oz

125 mL fresh parsley 1/2 cup

METHOD

1   In a large pot, cook the bacon strips over high heat until lightly caramelized. Remove the fat, leaving about 15 mL (1 tbsp) in the pot.

2   Add the onion, garlic, carrots and seasonings. Cook over medium heat for 5 minutes.

3   Add the tomato paste and continue cooking for another 2 minutes.

4   Add the water and bring to a boil. Simmer, partially covered, for 20 minutes.

5   Add the beans and pasta. Heat for another 3 minutes.

6   Garnish with chopped parsley.

Chicken Broth with Fava Beans and Pesto

6 to 8 servings

INGREDIENTS

500 g chicken thighs **1 lb**
2.5 L cold water **10 cups**
1 large onion, chopped **1**
2 stalks celery, chopped **2**
1 clove garlic **1**
1 mL dried thyme **1/4 tsp**
Pinch ground black pepper
2 bay leaves **2**
1 clove **1**
1 mL fennel seeds **1/4 tsp**
1 mL dried tarragon **1/4 tsp**
400 g fava beans, cooked and skinned, or one 540 mL (19-oz) can fava beans, drained, skinned and rinsed **2 cups**
45 mL pesto **3 tbsp**

Pesto (about 500 mL or 2 cups)
375 mL fresh basil **1 1/2 cups**
75 mL olive oil **1/3 cup**
125 mL fresh parsley **1/2 cup**
5 mL salt **1 tsp**
125 mL fresh spinach **1/2 cup**
Pinch cayenne pepper
5 cloves garlic **5**
Freshly ground pepper
60 mL fresh Parmesan **1/4 cup**

METHOD

PESTO

Place all the ingredients in a food processor and purée (3 to 5 minutes). Refrigerate.

BROTH

1 Place the chicken in a large pot and add cold water.

2 Bring to a boil. Reduce heat to low and skim off any foam that forms on the surface. Add all the ingredients except the beans and the pesto. Simmer over low heat for about 1 hour.

3 Drain the chicken thighs using a strainer, saving the cooking liquid. Cut the chicken thighs into small pieces and return them to the stock. Add the beans and the pesto.

4 Reheat without allowing to boil.

Tropical Mixed Bean Salsa

6 to 8 servings

COSTA RICA

Ideal with grilled fish or meat, nachos and quesadillas.

INGREDIENTS

1 mango, finely chopped 1

1 red onion, cut into medium slices 1

1 clove garlic, sliced 1

125 mL finely chopped fresh coriander 1/2 cup

125 mL sliced red pepper 1/2 cup

400 g cooked mixed beans or one 540 mL (19-oz) can mixed beans, rinsed and drained 2 cups

30 mL rice vinegar 2 tbsp

15 mL olive oil 1 tbsp

10 mL brown sugar 1/2 tbsp

2 mL salt 1/2 tsp

Pinch cayenne pepper

Freshly ground pepper

 METHOD

1 Mix together all finely chopped or sliced ingredients. Add the beans and seasonings.

2 Marinate in the refrigerator for at least 1 hour.

Pico de Gallo with Lentils and Melons

6 to 8 servings

MEXICO

A good accompaniment for grilled meat, tortillas and fried fish.

INGREDIENTS

375 mL chopped watermelon 1 1/2 cups

150 mL chopped honeydew melon 2/3 cup

150 mL chopped cantaloupe 2/3 cup

150 mL sliced red onion 2/3 cup

1 jalapeño pepper (optional) 1

1 clove garlic, chopped 1

400 g cooked lentils or one 540 mL (19-oz) can lentils, rinsed and drained 2 cups

30 mL vinegar 2 tbsp

15 mL olive oil 1 tbsp

Juice of 1 lime

10 mL brown sugar 2 tsp

Pinch salt

Pinch cayenne pepper

125 mL chopped fresh coriander 1/2 cup

METHOD

1 Mix together the fruits and vegetables and place in a large bowl. Add the lentils, vinegar, olive oil, lime juice, sugar and seasonings.

2 Marinate in the refrigerator for at least 1 hour.

Cajun Butter with Kidney Beans

This butter is excellent for grilling red meat.

INGREDIENTS

400 g cooked kidney beans or one 540 mL (19-oz) can cooked kidney beans, rinsed and drained **2 cups**

30 mL lemon juice **2 tbsp**

2 cloves garlic **2**

5 mL basil **1 tsp**

5 mL thyme **1 tsp**

5 mL oregano **1 tsp**

5 mL black pepper **1 tsp**

2 mL salt **1/2 tsp**

10 mL Worcestershire sauce **2 tsp**

45 mL Tabasco sauce **3 tbsp**

150 ml unsalted butter, cut in small cubes **2/3 cup**

METHOD

1 In a nonstick skillet, heat all the ingredients, except the butter, uncovered, over low heat for 5 minutes. Remove from heat.

2 Using a food processor, purée the entire mixture, gradually adding the butter cubes.

3 Pour into a bowl, cover with plastic wrap, flatten well and refrigerate for 24 hours.

Salads

Salads

Lupini Salad with Caraway Seeds

Chickpea Salad with Cardamom

Lentil and Wild Rice Salad

Warm Escarole Salad with Lima Beans and Smoked Bacon

Bean Sprout and Snow Pea Salad

Mixed Bean Salad

Black Bean and Citrus Salad

Tex-Mex Pinto Bean Salad

Italian-style Fava Bean Salad

Healthy Red Bean Salad

Lupini Salad with Caraway Seeds

To give the salad a different colour, replace the endives with radicchio and the red apples with a green or yellow variety.

4 to 6 servings

INGREDIENTS

500 g red apples (3 or 4) **1 lb**

400 g cooked lupini, skinned, or one 540 mL (19-oz) can lupini, rinsed, skinned and drained **2 cups**

Caraway dressing

500 g endives (6 to 8) **1 lb**

60 mL chopped chives (garnish) **1/4 cup**

Caraway Dressing

125 mL mayonnaise **1/2 cup**

75 mL plain yogurt, 0.1% m.f. **1/3 cup**

Juice of 1 orange

10 mL Dijon mustard **2 tsp**

2 mL ground caraway seeds **1/2 tsp**

Pinch ground white pepper

1 mL salt **1/4 tsp**

Pinch cayenne pepper

METHOD

DRESSING

Whisk together all ingredients for the dressing. Refrigerate.

SALAD

1 Core but do not peel the apples and cut into small cubes.

2 Place apple cubes in a large bowl; mix with the beans and two-thirds of the dressing.

3 Julienne the endives and line the plates. Drizzle with the remaining vinaigrette.

4 Add the apple and lupini salad, and garnish with chopped chives.

Chickpea Salad with Cardamom

To give the salad a Mediterranean flavour, add feta cheese.

INGREDIENTS

500 g cooked beets, sliced 1 lb

Cardamom dressing

45 mL chopped green onion 3 tbsp

45 mL chopped green pepper 3 tbsp

45 mL chopped red pepper 3 tbsp

45 mL chopped celery 3 tbsp

45 mL chopped carrot 3 tbsp

400 g cooked chickpeas or one 540 mL (19-oz) can chickpeas, rinsed and drained 2 cups

60 mL chopped fresh parsley (garnish) 1/4 cup

Cardamom Dressing

45 mL balsamic vinegar 3 tbsp

1 mL salt 1/4 tsp

1 mL oregano 1/4 tsp

1 mL paprika 1/4 tsp

1 mL ground cardamom 1/4 tsp

1 clove garlic 1

Pinch cayenne pepper

Freshly ground pepper

45 mL olive oil 3 tbsp

125 mL vegetable oil 1/2 cup

4 to 6 servings

METHOD

DRESSING

In a bowl, whisk together the balsamic vinegar and seasonings. Add both oils, whisking constantly. Refrigerate.

SALAD

1 Arrange the beet slices around the plates and drizzle with the vinaigrette.

2 Place the chopped vegetables in a large bowl. Add the chickpeas and the remaining dressing; mix well.

3 Garnish individual servings with parsley before serving.

Lentil and Wild Rice Salad

4 to 6 servings

INGREDIENTS

400 g cooked lentils or one 540 mL (19-oz) can lentils, rinsed and drained **2 cups**

250 mL cooked wild rice **1 cup**

125 mL grated carrot **1/2 cup**

60 mL chopped red pepper **1/4 cup**

60 mL chopped green onion **1/4 cup**

125 mL crushed peanuts (garnish) **1/2 cup**

Thai Dressing

180 mL vegetable oil **3/4 cup**

45 mL rice vinegar **3 tbsp**

5 mL peanut butter **1 tsp**

2 mL sesame oil **1/2 tsp**

2 mL soya oil **1/2 tsp**

Pinch salt

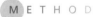 ETHOD

DRESSING

In a large bowl, blend all the ingredients except the oil. Whisk until the mixture is smooth. Add the oil a little at a time, whisking constantly. Refrigerate.

SALAD

1 Mix all the salad ingredients with the dressing. Marinate in the refrigerator for 1 hour.

2 Garnish the rims of the plates with exotic fruits such as pineapple, mango and kiwi, and arrange the salad in the centre of the plate.

Warm Escarole Salad with Lima Beans and Smoked Bacon

4 to 6 servings

INGREDIENTS

225 g smoked bacon, julienned **1/2 lb**

45 mL chopped green onion **3 tbsp**

15 mL dried tomatoes in oil, drained and chopped **1 tbsp**

10 mL brown sugar **2 tsp**

400 g large cooked lima beans, skinned, or one 540 mL (19-oz) can lima beans, rinsed, skinned and drained **2 cups**

1 clove garlic, chopped **1**

Pinch salt

Pinch cayenne pepper

Freshly ground pepper

15 mL balsamic vinegar **1 tbsp**

75 mL olive oil **1/3 cup**

500 g escarole **1 lb**

METHOD

1 Heat a large nonstick skillet over medium heat. Add the bacon strips and cook until golden.

2 Pour off the excess fat, leaving only about 15 mL (1 tbsp) in the skillet. Add the green onion, dried tomatoes and sugar. Cook for 2 to 3 minutes.

3 Add the beans and seasonings and heat thoroughly. Deglaze with balsamic vinegar. Add the olive oil. Mix well and allow to cool.

4 Arrange the escarole leaves on the plates. Add the bean and bacon mixture and drizzle with the warm dressing.

Bean Sprout and
Snow Pea Salad

Bean Sprout and Snow Pea Salad

4 to 6 servings

INGREDIENTS

1 large carrot, julienned 1

60 g julienned red onion 2 oz

60 g julienned red pepper 2 oz

500 g bean sprouts 1 lb

250 g snow peas, cut in half, blanched
but still crisp 8 oz

30 mL sesame seeds for garnish 2 tbsp

Sesame Oil Dressing

180 mL vegetable oil 3/4 cup

45 mL sesame oil 3 tbsp

15 mL balsamic vinegar 1 tbsp

30 mL soy sauce 2 tbsp

METHOD

DRESSING

In a bowl, whisk all the ingredients together.
Refrigerate.

SALAD

1 Mix together the julienned carrot, onion and red
pepper. Add the bean sprouts and snow peas.

2 Place on the plates, drizzle with the dressing and
garnish with sesame seeds.

Mixed Bean Salad

Mixed Bean Salad

Mesclun is a mixture of young lettuce shoots and leaves.

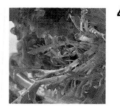

4 to 6 servings

INGREDIENTS

1 large tomato, seeded and chopped **1**

125 mL chopped green onion **1/2 cup**

800 g cooked mixed beans, or two **540 mL** (19-oz) cans mixed beans, rinsed and drained **4 cups**

Tarragon dressing

500 g mesclun **1 lb**

Tarragon Dressing

1/2 garlic clove, chopped **1/2**

125 mL chopped fresh tarragon **1/2 cup** or **10 mL** dried tarragon **2 tsp**

1 mL Dijon mustard **1/4 tsp**

Pinch salt

Pinch ground white pepper

Pinch cayenne pepper

Freshly ground pepper

60 mL balsamic vinegar **1/4 cup**

60 mL olive oil **1/4 cup**

125 mL vegetable oil **1/2 cup**

M ETHOD

DRESSING

In a large bowl, whisk together all ingredients except the oils. Mix well and slowly add the oils, whisking constantly. Refrigerate.

SALAD

1 In a salad bowl, combine the tomato, green onion and beans with half the dressing. Refrigerate for 1 hour.

2 Arrange the mesclun in the centre of the plates and drizzle with the remaining dressing. Place the marinated beans around the rim of the plate.

Black Bean and Citrus Salad

Variation: Add chunks of blue cheese and nuts.

INGREDIENTS

125 mL chopped green onion **1/2 cup**

125 mL chopped mushrooms **1/2 cup**

125 mL chopped red pepper **1/2 cup**

400 g cooked black beans, or one 540 mL (19-oz) can black beans, rinsed and drained **2 cups**

Tequila dressing

2 medium-sized pink grapefruits **2**

4 medium oranges **4**

6 clementines **6**

60 mL chopped chives (garnish) **1/4 cup**

1 lime (garnish) **1**

Tequila Dressing

125 mL citrus juice **1/2 cup**

125 mL olive oil **1/2 cup**

15 mL tequila **1 tbsp**

1 mL salt **1/4 tsp**

Pinch chili powder

1/2 garlic clove, chopped **1/2**

Freshly ground pepper

4 to 6 servings

METHOD

DRESSING

In a bowl, whisk all the ingredients together. Refrigerate.

SALAD

1 In a large bowl, mix the green onion, mushrooms and pepper. Add the beans and half the dressing. Marinate for 1 hour.

2 Meanwhile, peel the citrus fruits with a sharp knife in wide strips all around from top to bottom, taking care to remove all the white membrane of the peel. Slice the fruits so that they can be used for the bottom layer of the dish.

3 Top with the bean mixture and drizzle with the rest of the dressing. Garnish with chives and lime slices.

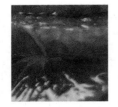

Tex-Mex Pinto Bean Salad

4 to 6 servings

INGREDIENTS

60 mL finely chopped green pepper **1/4 cup**

30 mL dried tomato in oil, drained and finely chopped **2 tbsp**

60 mL finely chopped celery **1/4 cup**

60 mL finely chopped fresh parsley **1/4 cup**

60 mL finely chopped fresh coriander **1/4 cup**

or **5 mL** dried coriander leaves **1 tsp**

400 g cooked pinto beans or one 540 mL (19-oz) can pinto beans, rinsed and drained **2 cups**

60 mL cooked corn kernels **1/4 cup**

Tex-Mex sauce

3 fresh tomatoes, sliced **3**

Tex-Mex Sauce

60 mL chopped onion **1/4 cup**

1 clove garlic **1**

60 mL vegetable oil **1/4 cup**

Juice of half a lime

2 mL Worcestershire sauce **1/2 tsp**

1 mL ground cumin **1/4 tsp**

Dash hot pepper sauce

1 mL salt **1/4 tsp**

Pinch brown sugar

Salt and pepper

METHOD

SAUCE

Blend all ingredients in a blender or food processor until smooth.

SALAD

1 In a large bowl, mix all the chopped ingredients for the salad. Add the beans, the corn and two-thirds of the Tex-Mex sauce. Marinate for 1 hour in the refrigerator.

2 Garnish the plates with tomatoes and drizzle with the remaining dressing. Arrange the bean salad in the centre.

Serve with tortillas or nachos.

Italian-style Fava Bean Salad

4 to 6 servings

INGREDIENTS

400 g large fava beans, cooked and skinned, or one 540 mL (19-oz) can fava beans, rinsed, skinned and drained **2 cups**

60 mL sliced green pepper **1/4 cup**

60 mL sliced red pepper **1/4 cup**

60 mL sliced fresh mushrooms **1/4 cup**

60 mL sliced celery **1/4 cup**

60 mL sliced carrots **1/4 cup**

60 mL sliced zucchini **1/4 cup**

1 tomato, finely chopped **1**

125 mL arugula (garnish) **1/2 cup**

60 mL grated Parmesan **1/4 cup**

Italian Dressing

60 mL balsamic vinegar **1/4 cup**

1 mL Dijon mustard **1/4 tsp**

1 clove garlic, chopped **1**

1 mL dried oregano **1/4 tsp**

1 mL dried basil **1/4 tsp**

1 mL paprika **1/4 tsp**

Pinch cayenne pepper

Pinch thyme

Pinch salt

Freshly ground pepper

125 mL olive oil **1/2 cup**

METHOD

DRESSING

In a salad bowl, whisk together all the dressing ingredients except the olive oil. Add the oil in a thin stream, whisking constantly.

SALAD

1 In a salad bowl, mix all the sliced vegetables and the chopped tomato. Add the dressing and refrigerate for at least 1 hour.

2 Place the salad on the plates, garnish with arugula and sprinkle with Parmesan.

Serve with polenta for a typical Italian meal.

Healthy Red Bean Salad

Variation: Use bean sprouts instead of watercress and white beans instead of red.

4 to 6 servings

INGREDIENTS

400 g cooked red beans or one 540 mL (19-oz) can cooked red beans, rinsed and drained **2 cups**

Curry yogurt sauce

2 carrots, julienned **2**

1/2 red pepper, julienned **1/2**

1 medium-sized mango, julienned **1**

500 g chopped watercress **2 cups**

Curry Yogurt Sauce

250 mL plain yogurt (0.1% m.f.) **1 cup**

1 banana, puréed **1**

2 mL Dijon mustard **1/2 tsp**

5 mL curry powder **1 tsp**

Pinch powdered turmeric

Pinch salt

1 clove garlic, chopped **1**

Freshly ground pepper

METHOD

SAUCE

Whisk together all ingredients. Refrigerate for 1 hour before serving.

SALAD

1 In a bowl, mix the red beans with half the sauce. Marinate for 30 minutes in the refrigerator.

2 In a salad bowl, add the julienned carrots and pepper, along with the mango. Add the watercress and the rest of the sauce; mix gently.

3 Place the salad in the centre and add the marinated beans around the rim of the plates.

Cold Appetizers

Cold Appetizers

Smoked Salmon Rosettes with Puy Lentils

Red Bean and Goat Cheese Rillettes

Prosciutto and Lima Beans with Port

Persillé of Mixed Beans with Chutney

Tomatoes Stuffed with Romano Beans

Scallops with Black Bean Salsa

Eggplant Caviar with Mussels and Lentil Coulis

Smoked Salmon Rosettes with Puy Lentils

4 to 6 servings

Julienned endive can be substituted for the mesclun.

INGREDIENTS

400 g cooked green Puy lentils **2 cups**
60 mL chopped green onion **1/4 cup**
60 mL chopped fresh parsley **1/4 cup**
Lemon marinade
350 g smoked salmon, sliced **12 oz**
250 g mesclun **9 oz**

Lemon Marinade
60 mL lemon juice **1/4 cup**
60 mL olive oil **1/4 cup**
125 mL vegetable oil **1/2 cup**
1 mL Dijon mustard **1/4 tsp**
1/2 garlic clove, chopped **1/2**
Pinch cayenne pepper
Pinch salt
Freshly ground pepper

METHOD

MARINADE

In a bowl, blend all ingredients and refrigerate.

ROSETTES

1 In a large bowl, combine the lentils, green onion and parsley with half the marinade. Marinate for 1 hour in the refrigerator.

2 To form rosettes with the salmon and mesclun, place salmon slices flat and roll them around a bouquet of mesclun. The salmon should form the shape of a flower.

3 Place the rosettes in the centre of the plates, drizzle with remaining marinade and place the marinated lentils around the rim.

Red Bean and Goat Cheese Rillettes

4 to 6 servings

INGREDIENTS

125 mL chopped green onion **1/2 cup**

1 clove garlic **1**

15 mL olive oil **1 tbsp**

200 g cooked red beans or half a 540 mL (19-oz) can red beans, rinsed and drained **1 cup**

2 mL chili powder **1/2 tsp**

1 mL salt **1/4 tsp**

Freshly ground pepper

500 g goat cheese, crumbled **1 lb**

60 g diced unsalted butter **1/4 cup**

60 mL chopped fresh rosemary **1/4 cup**

or **10 mL** dried rosemary **2 tsp**

METHOD

1 In a skillet, sauté the green onion and garlic in the olive oil for 2 to 3 minutes over medium heat. Add the beans, chili powder, salt and pepper, and cook for another 3 to 5 minutes. Remove from heat and let cool completely.

2 In a double boiler, melt the goat cheese until soft. Remove from heat and gradually add the butter, chopped rosemary and bean mixture, and stir gently.

3 Line a 25 cm by 10 cm (10- by 4-inch) mould with plastic wrap and pour in the mixture. Refrigerate for 24 hours.

Prosciutto and Lima Beans with Port

This appetizer may be served as part of an antipasto plate.

PORTUGAL

4 to 6 servings

INGREDIENTS

400 g cooked small lima beans or one 540 mL (19-oz) can lima beans, rinsed and drained **2 cups**

75 mL sliced red onion **1/3 cup**

500 g seedless red grapes, sliced in half **1 lb**

500 g thinly sliced prosciutto **1 lb**

Port Dressing

45 mL balsamic vinegar **3 tbsp**

45 mL port **3 tbsp**

125 mL olive oil **1/2 cup**

1 mL salt **1/4 tsp**

Pinch cayenne pepper

Freshly ground pepper

METHOD

1 In a bowl, whisk together all the ingredients of the dressing. Refrigerate.

2 In a salad bowl, mix the beans, onion slices and grapes with two-thirds of the dressing. Marinate for 30 minutes in the refrigerator.

3 Garnish the plates with prosciutto slices and drizzle with the remaining dressing. Place the bean and grape mixture in the centre of the plates.

Persillé of Mixed Beans with Apricot Chutney

METHOD

4 to 6 servings

INGREDIENTS

250 g boneless chicken breast, cubed **1/2 lb**

175 mL 35% cream **3/4 cup**

15 mL olive oil **1 tbsp**

60 mL chopped green onion **1/4 cup**

1 clove garlic, chopped **1**

Salt and pepper to taste

400 g cooked mixed beans or one 540 mL (19-oz) can mixed beans, rinsed and drained **2 cups**

60 mL chopped fresh parsley **1/4 cup**

Apricot Cardamom Chutney

250 g dried apricots **1/2 lb**

125 mL boiling water or hot chicken stock **1/2 cup**

15 mL olive oil **1 tbsp**

250 mL thinly sliced onion **1 cup**

1 mL ground cardamom **1/4 tsp**

10 mL brown sugar **2 tsp**

1 mL salt **1/4 tsp**

Freshly ground pepper

15 mL balsamic vinegar **1 tbsp**

PERSILLÉ

1 Preheat oven to 180ºC (350ºF).

2 In a food processor, purée the chicken and 35% cream until smooth. Refrigerate.

3 In a skillet, cook the green onion, garlic and beans in the olive oil over medium heat for 3 to 5 minutes. Add salt and pepper, and allow to cool.

4 In a bowl, gently mix together the puréed chicken, green onion, garlic, beans and parsley.

5 Line a 25 cm by 10 cm (10- by 4-inch) mould with plastic wrap. Pour in the mixture, set the mould in a dish of hot water and cook at 180ºC (350ºF) for 45 minutes. Cool before unmoulding.

CHUTNEY

1 Soak the dried apricots in boiling water or hot chicken stock for 30 minutes. Drain the apricots, reserving the liquid.

2 In a pot, cook the onion, cardamom, brown sugar, salt and pepper in the olive oil, over medium heat, until the mixture begins to caramelize.

3 Add the apricots and cook, uncovered, for another 2 to 3 minutes.

4 Deglaze with the balsamic vinegar. Add the water or stock used to soak the apricots. Simmer for another 5 minutes. Remove from heat.

Serve the persillé chilled, with warm chutney.

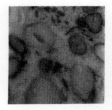

Tomatoes Stuffed with Romano Beans

4 to 6 servings

Tomatoes Stuffed with Romano Beans

INGREDIENTS

125 mL pine nuts **1/2 cup**

60 mL sliced green onions **1/4 cup**

60 mL sliced carrots **1/4 cup**

60 mL sliced celery **1/4 cup**

60 mL sliced red pepper **1/4 cup**

250 g portobello or oyster mushrooms **1 cup**

15 mL olive oil **1 tbsp**

400 g cooked romano beans or one 540 mL (19-oz) can romano beans, rinsed and drained **2 cups**

60 mL chopped fresh parsley **1/4 cup**

1 kg tomatoes (4 to 6 medium-sized) **2 lb**

Walnut Oil Dressing

60 mL red wine vinegar **1/4 cup**

175 mL walnut oil **3/4 cup**

Pinch salt

Pinch ground white pepper

METHOD

DRESSING

In a small bowl, whisk together all the ingredients and refrigerate.

STUFFED TOMATOES

1 In a nonstick skillet, toast the pine nuts for 5 minutes over medium heat until they start to turn golden. Remove from heat and reserve.

2 Wash the mushrooms and cut into bean-sized pieces.

3 In a large pot, heat the olive oil over medium heat and cook the vegetables for 2 to 3 minutes. Add the mushrooms and beans. Add salt and pepper to taste and cook for 2 to 3 more minutes. Remove from heat and allow to cool completely.

4 Place in a salad bowl and mix in the pine nuts and two-thirds of the dressing.

5 Cut off the tops of the tomatoes and save to be used as "lids" once the tomatoes are stuffed.

6 Scoop out the contents of the tomatoes and fill with the mushroom/bean mixture, replace the "lids" and drizzle with the remaining dressing.

Serve the tomatoes on a bed of salad greens.

Scallops with Black Bean Salsa

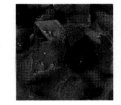

4 to 6 servings

INGREDIENTS

500 g large scallops **1 lb**
180 mL lime juice (4 or 5 limes) **3/4 cup**
1 mL salt **1/4 tsp**
5 mL jalapeño pepper (optional) **1 tsp**
Freshly ground pepper

Black Bean Salsa
400 g cooked black beans or one 540 mL (19-oz) can black beans, rinsed and drained **2 cups**
125 mL finely diced mango **1/2 cup**
125 mL chopped red onion **1/2 cup**
1 clove garlic, chopped **1**
60 mL chopped fresh coriander **1/4 cup** or **5 mL** dried coriander **1 tsp**
30 mL red wine vinegar **2 tbsp**
15 mL olive oil **1 tbsp**
5 mL brown sugar **1 tsp**
1 mL salt **1/4 tsp**
Pinch cayenne pepper
Freshly ground pepper

METHOD

SCALLOPS

1 Slice the scallops in half lengthwise and marinate in the lime juice with the seasonings for 20 to 30 minutes or until the scallops are slightly blanched. Remove from the marinade and refrigerate. Save the marinade in a separate container and refrigerate.

2 On a plate, form a crown of scallops and place the salsa in the centre. Drizzle the scallops with a little marinade.

BLACK BEAN SALSA

In a large bowl, mix all the ingredients and refrigerate for at least 1 hour before serving.

Eggplant Caviar with Mussels and Lentil Coulis

4 to 6 servings

15 mL olive oil **1 tbsp**

60 mL chopped celery **1/4 cup**

125 mL chopped onion **1/2 cup**

125 mL chopped carrot **1/2 cup**

1 leek, chopped (white part only) **1**

1 mL coriander seeds **1/4 tsp**

1 mL fennel seeds **1/4 tsp**

Pinch dried thyme

2 bay leaves **2**

Freshly ground pepper

1 kg mussels **2 lb**

45 mL water **3 tbsp**

Eggplant Caviar

60 mL water **1/4 cup**

15 mL olive oil **1 tbsp**

1 kg eggplant, cubed **2 lb**

500 g fresh tomatoes, chopped **1 lb**

60 mL balsamic vinegar **1/4 cup**

60 mL chopped green onion **1/4 cup**

2 cloves garlic, chopped **2**

60 mL chopped fresh parsley **1/4 cup**

1 mL salt **1/4 tsp**

Pinch cayenne pepper

Freshly ground pepper

Lentil Mint Coulis

400 g cooked green lentils or one 540 mL (19-oz) can lentils, rinsed and drained **2 cups**

125 mL fresh mint **1/2 cup**

2 cloves garlic **2**

5 mL Dijon mustard **1 tsp**

60 mL chopped green onion **1/4 cup**

Juice of half a lemon

75 mL olive oil **1/3 cup**

75 mL cold cooking liquid from mussels **1/3 cup**

1 mL salt **1/4 tsp**

Pinch cayenne pepper

Freshly ground pepper

M E T H O D

MUSSELS

1 In a large pot, heat the olive oil over medium heat. Cook the vegetables with the coriander, fennel, thyme, bay leaves and pepper, uncovered, for 3 to 5 minutes.

2 Add the mussels and water; cover and cook until the mussels open (about 3 to 5 minutes).

3 Shuck the mussels, place them in a bowl and add lemon juice. Place in refrigerator. Save a few mussels for garnish.

CAVIAR

1 Heat oven to 230°C (450°F).

2 Grease a baking sheet with olive oil.

3 Peel and cut the eggplant into 2.5 cm (1-inch) cubes. Place on the baking sheet, sprinkle with water, cover with aluminum foil and bake at 230°C (450°F) for 1 hour.

4 Remove the eggplant slices from the oven and leave to drain in a sieve for 30 minutes. In the meantime, chop the tomatoes, green onion, garlic and parsley, and place in a salad bowl. Add the remaining seasonings and marinate while you mash the eggplant. Mix the mashed eggplant with the other vegetables. Refrigerate.

LENTIL MINT COULIS

In a food processor or blender, blend all ingredients until a smooth mixture is obtained. Strain and refrigerate.

FINISHING TOUCHES

1 Mix about 10 mussels with 1 portion of caviar. From this mixture, make dumplings of 30 mL (2 tbsp) each.

2 Place 2 to 3 dumplings on each plate and drizzle with lentil mint sauce.

The eggplant caviar can be made the day before it is served.

Hot Appetizers

Hot Appetizers

Escargot Bundles with Garlic Cream

Confit of Duck on a Bed of Bean Sprouts

Frogs' Legs with Fava Beans

Gratin of Chickpeas and Goat Cheese

Chicken Livers with Pinto Beans

Oyster and Mung Bean Stew

Aiguillettes of Duck with Bean Sprouts

Lupini and Chipolata Gratin

Escargot Bundles with Garlic Cream

It is easier to work with filo if the unfolded sheets are placed on a piece of plastic wrap, covered with a second sheet of plastic wrap and a dampened dish towel. Remove only one sheet of filo at a time.

Makes **18**

INGREDIENTS

Filling

30 mL olive oil **2 tbsp**

48 escargots, rinsed and drained **48**

15 mL chopped green onion **1 tbsp**

1/2 clove garlic, chopped **1/2**

400 g cooked flageolets or one 540 mL (19-oz) can flageolets, rinsed and drained **2 cups**

2 mL dried basil **1/2 tsp**

2 mL paprika **1/2 tsp**

1 mL dried thyme **1/4 tsp**

1 mL salt **1/4 tsp**

Pinch cayenne pepper

200 g blue or goat cheese, crumbled **7 oz**

Garlic Cream

6 cloves garlic **6**

250 mL milk **1 cup**

500 mL 35% cream **2 cups**

60 mL soy sauce **1/4 cup**

Pinch salt

Pinch ground white pepper

Bundles

18 leaves filo dough **18**

125 mL melted butter **1/2 cup**

METHOD

GARNISH

1 In a large skillet, heat the oil over high heat and sauté the escargots, green onion and garlic for 2 minutes.

2 Add the flageolets, basil, paprika, thyme, salt and cayenne, and cook over medium heat for 5 more minutes.

3 Remove from heat and let cool completely. Refrigerate.

GARLIC CREAM

1 In a small pot, blanch the garlic in 250 mL (1 cup) milk, that is, bring to a boil and remove from heat. Rinse the garlic under cold water and discard the milk. Repeat the operation a second time.

2 Place the blanched garlic in a small pot and pour in the cream and soy sauce. Season and bring to a boil, uncovered. Simmer over medium heat for 5 minutes or until the sauce has been reduced by one-third. Remove from heat and allow to cool for 10 to 15 minutes.

3 In a blender or food processor, blend the sauce for about 3 minutes. Strain and set aside. Keep warm.

BUNDLES

1 Heat the oven to 190°C (375°F).

2 To form a bundle, cut 1 sheet of filo dough into 4 equal sections; brush each one with melted butter and place one on top of another so that the corners do not line up.

3 Place 60 mL (4 tbsp) of escargot-flageolet filling in the middle and sprinkle with cheese. Bring the corners of the filo together over the filling and twist to form a small bundle. Repeat with the remaining dough and filling.

4 Place the bundles on a cookie sheet and bake at 190°C (375°F) for 10 minutes or until they are golden.

5 Pour a small amount of garlic cream over the bundles. Serve as an appetizer on a plate garnished with lettuce leaves, 2 to 3 bundles per serving.

Confit of Duck on a Bed of Bean Sprouts

INGREDIENTS

30 mL olive oil **2 tbsp**
1 kg duck legs (4 to 6) **2 lb**
30 mL chopped green onion **2 tbsp**
Pinch salt
Freshly ground pepper
15 mL rice vinegar **1 tbsp**
400 g carrots, julienned **14 oz**
400 g bean sprouts **14 oz**
Sesame Dressing
45 mL sesame seeds **3 tbsp**

Sesame Dressing
125 mL vegetable oil **1/2 cup**
60 mL rice vinegar **1/4 cup**
30 mL sesame oil **2 tbsp**
Pinch salt
10 mL brown sugar **2 tsp**

4 to 6 servings

METHOD

DRESSING

n a small pot, whisk together all the ingredients and cook over low heat. Set aside. Keep warm.

DUCK LEGS

1 In a large skillet, heat the olive oil over medium heat, arrange the duck legs skin side down and cook for 5 to 8 minutes.

2 Add the green onion, salt and pepper, and cook for 2 to 3 more minutes over low heat. Turn the duck legs over and deglaze with rice vinegar. Remove from heat and keep warm.

3 In a bowl, mix the carrots and bean sprouts and arrange in the middle of the plates. Add the duck legs and drizzle with warm dressing. Sprinkle with sesame seeds.

Frogs' Legs with Fava Beans

Variation: Large shrimps can be substituted for the frogs' legs.

4 to 6 servings

INGREDIENTS

30 mL olive oil **2 tbsp**

4 dozen frogs' legs, marinated **4**

125 mL chopped green onion **1/2 cup**

1 clove garlic, chopped **1**

60 mL chopped red pepper **1/4 cup**

60 mL chopped yellow pepper **1/4 cup**

400 g cooked fava beans or one 540 mL (19-oz) can fava beans, rinsed and drained **2 cups**

250 mL coconut milk **1 cup**

1 mL salt **1/4 tsp**

Freshly ground pepper

60 mL chopped fresh coriander **1/4 cup**
or **2 mL** dried coriander **1/2 tsp**

Marinade for Frogs' Legs

30 mL olive oil **2 tbsp**

30 mL Pastis or Pernod **2 tbsp**

5 mL chopped lemon grass **1 tsp**

1 mL paprika **1/4 tsp**

1 mL curry powder **1/4 tsp**

1 mL salt **1/4 tsp**

1 clove garlic, chopped **1**

Freshly ground pepper

METHOD

MARINADE

In a large bowl, whisk all ingredients together. Add the frogs' legs and stir gently. Marinate in the refrigerator for 2 hours.

FROGS' LEGS

1 In a large skillet, heat the olive oil over high heat. Sear the frogs' legs for 2 minutes, turn over gently and reduce heat to medium; continue cooking for another 3 to 4 minutes or until the meat separates easily from the bone. Remove the legs from the skillet and keep warm.

2 In the same skillet, cook the green onion, garlic and peppers for 3 minutes over low heat.

3 Add the fava beans and coconut milk and bring to a boil. Lower the heat, season with salt and pepper, and simmer for 5 minutes. Remove from heat and add the coriander.

4 Arrange the beans on deep plates, add the frogs' legs and cover with the coconut milk.

Gratin of Chickpeas and Goat Cheese

4 to 6 servings

INGREDIENTS

15 mL olive oil **1 tbsp**

60 mL chopped green onion **1/4 cup**

1 clove garlic, chopped **1**

400 g cooked chickpeas or one 540 mL (19-oz) can chickpeas, rinsed and drained **2 cups**

2 mL chili powder **1/2 tsp**

1 mL ground cumin **1/4 tsp**

1 mL dried oregano **1/4 tsp**

Pinch dried thyme

Pinch cayenne pepper

Pinch salt

Freshly ground pepper

250 g chorizo (a dry Spanish sausage), thinly sliced **9 oz**

60 mL chopped fresh parsley **1/4 cup**

180 mL crushed tomatoes **3/4 cup**

250 g goat cheese **9 oz**

METHOD

1 In a large skillet, heat the olive oil over medium heat. Cook the green onion and garlic for 2 minutes.

2 Add the chickpeas, seasonings and sliced chorizo; cook for 3 minutes.

3 Add the crushed tomatoes and parsley. Stir and reheat thoroughly. Remove from heat.

4 Place the mixture in the middle of the plates and cover with goat cheese. Place under the grill of the oven briefly until the goat cheese has softened a little.

Chicken Livers with Pinto Beans

4 to 6 servings

INGREDIENTS

30 mL olive oil **2 tbsp**

1 kg chicken livers, cleaned **2 lb**

225 g Shiitake or oyster mushrooms, minced **8 oz**

60 mL chopped green onion **1/4 cup**

1 clove garlic, chopped **1**

2 mL fresh ginger **1/2 tsp**

400 g cooked pinto beans or one 540 mL (19-oz) can pinto beans, rinsed and drained **2 cups**

30 mL soy sauce **2 tbsp**

180 mL 35% cream **3/4 cup**

60 mL butter **1/4 cup**

60 mL chopped fresh parsley **1/4 cup**

METHOD

1 In a large skillet, heat half the olive oil over high heat. Sear the livers for 2 minutes. Lower the heat and continue cooking for 3 minutes. Remove from heat, place the livers in a bowl and keep warm.

2 In the same skillet, add the rest of the olive oil and sauté the mushrooms, green onion, garlic and ginger for 3 minutes at medium heat. Add the beans and cook for another 3 minutes.

3 Deglaze with the soy sauce and add the 35% cream. Bring to a boil over high heat for 1 minute to reduce.

4 Remove from heat and gradually add the butter, stirring gently. Sprinkle with chopped parsley.

5 Place the bean-mushroom mixture in the middle of the plates; surround with chicken livers and cover with sauce.

Oyster and Mung Bean Stew

Oyster and Mung Bean Stew

INGREDIENTS

15 mL olive oil 1 tbsp
75 mL sliced carrots 1/3 cup
75 mL sliced celery 1/3 cup
75 mL sliced red pepper 1/3 cup
30 mL sliced green onions 2 tbsp
500 g cooked mung beans 2 cups
36 fresh oysters, shucked 36
500 mL saffron-flavoured vegetables 2 cups
1 mL salt 1/4 tsp
Freshly ground pepper
60 mL dill, chopped 1/4 cup
or 2 mL dried dill 1/2 tsp

Saffron-flavoured Vegetables (1 L - 4 cups)

125 mL chopped onion 1/2 cup
125 mL chopped carrot 1/2 cup
1 leek, chopped (white and green parts) 1
60 mL chopped white mushrooms 1/4 cup
60 mL chopped celery 1/4 cup
60 mL chopped parsley 1/4 cup
1 mL fennel seeds 1/4 tsp
1 mL coriander seeds 1/4 tsp
A few whole peppercorns
Pinch dried thyme
2 bay leaves 2
1/4 mL saffron 1/4 tsp
15 mL olive oil 1 tbsp
1.5 L water 6 cups

METHOD

4 to 6 servings

OYSTER STEW

1 In a medium pot, heat the olive oil over medium heat. Sauté the sliced vegetables for 3 to 5 minutes.

2 Add the mung beans, shucked oysters and the saffron-flavoured vegetables.

3 Bring to a boil, lower the heat and simmer for 2 minutes. Add salt and pepper.

4 Remove from heat. Sprinkle with chopped dill.

VEGETABLES

1 In a large pot, heat the olive oil over medium heat. Cook all the vegetables, with spices, for 5 to 8 minutes.

2 Add water, bring to a boil, and simmer, uncovered, for 15 to 20 minutes or until the liquid has been reduced by one-third.

3 Remove from heat and filter through a sieve. Refrigerate.

The leftover vegetables may be frozen in an airtight container.

Aiguillettes of Duck with Bean Sprouts

INGREDIENTS

30 mL olive oil 2 tbsp

500 g duck fillets 1 lb

120 g julienned carrot 4 oz

120 g julienned leek (white part only) 4 oz

120 g julienned red pepper 4 oz

500 g bean sprouts 1 lb

125 mL canned whole corn kernels 1/2 cup

1 clove garlic, chopped 1

Pinch cayenne pepper

Salt and pepper

180 mL cashew pieces 3/4 cup

Raspberry Dressing

60 mL raspberry vinegar 1/4 cup

60 mL olive oil 1/4 cup

60 mL walnut oil 1/4 cup

60 mL vegetable oil 1/4 cup

Pinch salt

Pinch ground white pepper

2 mL Dijon mustard 1/2 tsp

4 to 6 servings

METHOD

DRESSING

In a bowl, whisk together all the ingredients until a smooth mixture is obtained. Refrigerate until serving.

AIGUILLETTES

1 In a heavy skillet, heat half the olive oil over high heat and sauté the duck fillets for 2 to 3 minutes (or according to preference). Remove from heat and keep warm.

2 In the same hot skillet, add the remaining olive oil and sauté the julienned carrot, leek and red pepper for 2 minutes.

3 Add the bean sprouts, corn and chopped garlic to the skillet and cook for 3 more minutes. Season. Lower the heat, add the cashews and half the dressing; cook for 1 more minute.

4 Divide the bean sprouts and vegetables into servings on the plates. Top with the aiguillettes and drizzle with the remaining dressing.

Lupini and Chipolata Gratin

To give this dish a Moroccan flavour, substitute chickpeas and merguez for the chipolatas and lupini.

4 to 6 servings

INGREDIENTS

15 mL olive oil **1 tbsp**

250 g chipolata sausages, cut into 1 cm (1/2-inch) rounds **1/2 lb**

125 mL chopped onion **1/2 cup**

375 mL fresh tomatoes, seeded and chopped **1 1/2 cups**

400 g lupini, cooked and skinned, or one 540 mL (19-oz) can lupini, rinsed, skinned and drained **2 cups**

1 clove garlic, chopped **1**

60 mL dried tomatoes rehydrated in oil, drained and chopped **1/4 cup**

1 mL salt **1/4 tsp**

Freshly ground pepper

Pinch sugar

60 mL chopped fresh basil **1/4 cup** or **5 mL** dried basil **1 tsp**

180 mL freshly grated Parmesan **3/4 cup**

METHOD

1 In a skillet, heat the olive oil over medium heat and sauté the sausages for 3 to 5 minutes or until cooked.

2 Remove from the skillet and keep warm.

3 In the same skillet, caramelize the onion for 3 or 4 minutes. Add the chopped tomatoes, lupini, garlic and dried tomatoes. Season and cook, uncovered, for 5 minutes.

4 Return the chipolatas to the skillet and add the chopped basil. Cook for 1 minute and remove from heat.

5 Place in the middle of the plates, sprinkle with Parmesan and place under the grill of the oven at for 1 minute.

Main Dishes

Main Dishes

Lobster Medallions with Mung Beans

Grilled Salmon with Semolina and Green Lentils

Scallops with Pigeon Peas and Coulis

Shark Brochettes with Small Broad Beans

Fried Sardines with Concassé of Lupini

Tuna with White Bean Quenelles

Pan-fried Shripms and Lima Beans with Hot Pepper Oil

Skate Wings with Sautéed Bean Sprouts

Chicken Supreme with Red Bean Compote

Grilled Pork Chops with Green Split Pea Purée

Veal Medallions with Small Red Beans and Duxelles

Braised Rabbit with Black Beans

Quail Duo on a bed of Lentils

Turkey Paupiettes with Lima Beans

Lamb Chops with Provençal-style Chickpeas

Tournedos with Mixed Beans Ratatouille

Veal Kidneys with Black-eyed Peas

Magrets of Duck with Kiwis and Snow Peas

Leg of Wild Boar with Mousseline of Yellow Split Peas

Loin of Deer with Flageolets

Lobster Medallions with Mung Beans

INGREDIENTS

1 kg lobster tails **2 lb**

2 L water **8 cups**

Pinch salt

Marinade

30 mL olive oil **2 tbsp**

10 mL Dijon mustard **2 tsp**

1 clove garlic, chopped **1**

5 mL ground allspice **1 tsp**

2 mL dried thyme **1/2 tsp**

10 mL dried basil **2 tsp**

Pinch cayenne pepper

Freshly ground pepper

Mung Beans

15 mL olive oil **1 tbsp**

15 mL chopped green onion **1 tbsp**

1 clove garlic, chopped **1**

125 mL chopped red pepper **1/2 cup**

125 mL chopped yellow pepper **1/2 cup**

250 g sliced Shiitake or oyster mushrooms **1 cup**

500 g cooked mung beans **2 cups**

60 mL soy sauce **1/4 cup**

250 mL 35% cream **1 cup**

Salt and pepper

60 mL chopped fresh parsley **1/4 cup**

4 to 6 servings

METHOD

In a large pot, bring 2 L (8 cups) of salted water to a boil. Immerse the lobster tails in the water. Once the water has returned to a boil, cook the lobster tails for 5 minutes, Remove from the water and allow to cool. Remove meat from the shell.

MARINADE

Cut the lobster meat into medallions of about 1 cm (1/2 inch). In a bowl, blend all the ingredients and place the medallions on top of the mixture. Marinate for 12 hours in the refrigerator.

MUNG BEANS

1 In a 2 L (8-cup) saucepan, heat the olive oil over high heat and cook the green onion, garlic and peppers for 2 to 3 minutes. Add the mushrooms and continue cooking for 2 minutes. Add the beans and cook for another 2 minutes.

2 Deglaze with the soy sauce; pour in the 35% cream, season and bring to a boil. Lower heat to medium and reduce the sauce for 2 to 3 minutes. Remove from heat, sprinkle with parsley and keep warm.

SERVING

In a nonstick skillet, heat the medallions over medium heat for 1 for 2 minutes per side. Arrange the bean and mushroom mixture on the plates and top with the medallions.

Grilled Salmon with Green Lentils

Grilled Salmon
with Green
Lentils

4 to 6 servings

INGREDIENTS

1 kg skinned salmon fillets **2 lb**

30 mL coriander oil **2 tbsp**

Pinch salt

Freshly ground pepper

Coriander Oil

125 mL olive oil **1/2 cup**

60 mL fresh coriander, chopped **1/4 cup**

Juice of half a lemon

1/2 clove garlic, chopped **1/2**

Pinch cayenne pepper

Pinch salt

Freshly ground pepper

Semolina

250 mL medium semolina **1 cup**

10 mL curry powder **2 tsp**

30 mL olive oil **2 tbsp**

250 mL hot water or hot vegetable stock **1 cup**

1 clove garlic, chopped **1**

60 mL green onions, chopped **1/4 cup**

30 mL dried tomatoes in oil, drained and chopped **2 tbsp**

250 g cooked green lentils **1 cup**

Pinch cayenne pepper

Pinch salt

Freshly ground pepper

METHOD

1 Brush the salmon fillets with coriander oil; season with salt and pepper.

2 Grill the salmon for 3 to 4 minutes per side on a very hot barbecue or under the broiler.

3 Keep warm.

CORIANDER OIL

Using a blender or food processor, blend all ingredients for 3 minutes. Strain through a sieve. Set aside at room temperature.

SEMOLINA

1 In a large bowl, thoroughly blend the semolina, curry powder and 15 mL (1 tbsp) olive oil. Add the hot water or vegetable stock.

2 Stir, cover with plastic wrap and leave at room temperature for 1 hour.

3 Uncover and fluff the semolina with a fork. Refrigerate.

GREEN LENTILS

1 In a medium-sized skillet, heat the remaining olive oil over high heat and sauté the garlic, green onions and dried tomatoes for 2 minutes.

2 Add the lentils and seasonings. Continue cooking over medium heat for another 2 or 3 minutes, until the lentils are dry. Remove from heat and allow to cool.

3 In a large salad bowl, mix the semolina and lentils; serve hot or cold. If serving hot, reheat in the microwave.

4 Place the semolina and lentil mixture in the middle of the plates and arrange the salmon over top. Drizzle with the remaining coriander oil.

Scallops with Pigeon Peas and Coulis

4 to 6 servings

INGREDIENTS

15 mL olive oil **1 tbsp**

700 g large scallops, halved lengthwise **1 1/2 lb**

10 mL unsalted butter **2 tsp**

1 clove garlic **1**

175 mL oyster mushrooms **3/4 cup**

500 g cooked pigeon peas **2 cups**

Salt and pepper

60 mL fresh parsley, chopped **1/4 cup**

Black Olive Coulis

15 mL olive oil **1 tbsp**

400 g black olives, pitted and drained **14 oz**

15 mL chopped green onion **1 tbsp**

Pinch fennel seed

Pinch dried thyme

Pinch salt

Pinch cayenne pepper

1 bay leaf **1**

Freshly ground pepper

125 mL water or vegetable stock **1/2 cup**

METHOD

BLACK OLIVE COULIS

1 In a medium-sized saucepan, heat the olive oil and cook all the ingredients for the coulis over low heat for 5 minutes.

2 Add water or vegetable stock and bring to a boil over high heat. Reduce the heat, cover and simmer for 20 minutes. Remove from heat and allow to cool for 10 minutes.

3 Purée in a food processor or blender. Serve hot or cold.

SCALLOPS

1 In a large skillet, sear the scallops in very hot olive oil for 1 minute per side. They must not be overcooked.

2 Remove from the skillet and keep warm.

3 In the same skillet, add the butter and sauté the garlic and oyster mushrooms for 2 to 3 minutes.

4 Add the pigeon peas, season and cook for another 3 minutes over medium heat. Remove from heat and sprinkle with parsley.

5 Place the pea and mushroom mixture in the middle of the plates and pile the scallops around the periphery to form a crown. Top with the hot black olive coulis.

Shark Brochettes with Small Broad Beans

For an exotic touch, substitute mango for the pineapple.

4 to 6 servings

INGREDIENTS

Brochettes

1 kg shark fillets, cleaned and cut into 2.5 cm (1-inch) cubes **2 lb**

Marinade

125 mL soy sauce **1/2 cup**

30 mL honey **2 tbsp**

10 mL chopped fresh ginger **2 tsp**

2 cloves garlic, chopped **2**

5 mL Dijon mustard **1 tsp**

125 mL vegetable oil **1/2 cup**

45 mL sesame oil **3 tbsp**

1 mL hot pepper sauce **1/4 tsp**

Broad Beans and Pineapple

400 g cooked small broad beans, skinned, or two 540 mL (19-oz) cans broad beans, rinsed and drained **2 cups**

250 mL chopped pineapple **1 cup**

125 mL chopped red onion **1/2 cup**

125 mL chopped red pepper **1/2 cup**

60 mL chopped fresh coriander **1/4 cup** or **2 mL** dried coriander **1/2 tsp**

45 mL rice vinegar **3 tbsp**

125 mL olive oil **1/2 cup**

10 mL brown sugar **2 tsp**

1 mL salt **1/4 tsp**

Freshly ground pepper

METHOD

MARINADE

In a bowl, whisk together all the marinade ingredients. Add the shark cubes and marinate for 6 hours in the refrigerator.

BROAD BEANS AND PINEAPPLE

In a large salad bowl, combine all ingredients 1 hour before serving.

Refrigerate.

BROCHETTES

1 Preheat the barbecue to medium hot or the oven broiler to medium heat. Place the brochettes on the grill or on a baking sheet under the broiler. Grill or broil for about 8 minutes, turning regularly, taking care not to overcook them.

2 Place the brochettes on a bed of broad beans and pineapple.

Fried Sardines with Concassé of Lupini

4 to 6 servings

INGREDIENTS

2 eggs 2

500 mL milk **2 cups**

250 mL flour **1 cup**

1 kg fresh sardine fillets **2 lb**

250 mL shelled almonds, coarsely chopped **1 cup**

500 mL vegetable oil **2 cups**

Concassé

15 mL olive oil **1 tbsp**

125 mL chopped onion **1/2 cup**

2 cloves garlic, chopped **2**

400 mL cooked lupini, skinned, or one 540 mL (19-oz) can lupini, rinsed, skinned and drained **2 cups**

60 mL white wine **1/4 cup**

375 mL fresh tomatoes, seeded and chopped **1 1/2 cups**

Pinch salt

Pinch brown sugar

Pinch cayenne pepper

Freshly ground pepper

10 leaves fresh basil, chopped **10**

METHOD

1 In a medium-sized bowl, beat the eggs and milk.

2 Dredge the sardine fillets in the flour and dip one by one in the egg and milk mixture. Remove from the mixture, drain and roll in the almonds.

3 In a skillet, heat the oil over high heat 180°C (425°F) measured with a thermometer and fry the fillets for about 3 minutes.

4 Remove from the skillet, drain on paper towels and keep warm.

CONCASSÉ

1 In a large skillet, heat the oil and sauté the onion, garlic and lupini over medium heat for 3 minutes.

2 Deglaze with white wine and add the tomatoes and seasoning. Bring to a boil, reduce the heat and simmer, uncovered, for 2 minutes.

3 Remove from heat and add the chopped basil.

4 Divide the concassé among the plates and top with very hot sardines.

Tuna with White Bean Quenelles

Tuna with White
Bean Quenelles

4 to 6 servings

INGREDIENTS

1 kg fresh tuna, cut into 4 to 6 pieces **2 lb**

Marinade

60 mL fish sauce **1/4 cup**

60 mL sesame oil **1/4 cup**

60 mL molasses **1/4 cup**

125 mL water **1/2 cup**

Quenelles

15 mL olive oil **1 tbsp**

10 mL green onions, chopped **2 tsp**

800 g cooked white kidney beans or two 540 mL (19-oz) cans white kidney beans, rinsed and drained **4 cups**

Salt and pepper

125 mL chopped chives **1/2 cup**

METHOD

MARINADE

1 In a bowl, blend all the marinade ingredients. Add the tuna pieces, cover with plastic wrap and marinate 6 hours in the refrigerator.

2 Remove the tuna from the marinade. Refrigerate.

3 Boil the marinade, uncovered, for 1 minute. Remove from heat, strain and keep warm.

QUENELLES

1 In a large skillet, heat the olive oil and sauté the green onions for 2 minutes. Add the white beans. Season and cook for 3 minutes.

2 Remove from heat and purée the beans in a food processor. Keep warm.

3 Add the chopped chives. Set aside and keep warm.

4 When ready to serve, shape the mixture into quenelles using 30 to 45 mL (2 to 3 tbsp) per quenelle.

TUNA

1 Preheat the oven to 220°C (425°F). Line a baking sheet with aluminum foil. Place the tuna pieces on the sheet and bake for 8 minutes.

2 Place the tuna on the plates. Add 2 or 3 quenelles and drizzle with a little warm marinade.

Pan-fried Shrimps and Lima Beans with Hot Pepper Oil

4 to 6 servings

INGREDIENTS

45 mL hot pepper oil (see recipe below) 3 tbsp

700 g large shrimps 1 1/2 lb

125 mL chopped green onion 1/2 cup

125 mL chopped green pepper 1/2 cup

125 mL chopped red pepper 1/2 cup

400 mL large cooked lima beans, or one
 540 mL (19-oz) can lima beans, rinsed
 and drained 2 cups

Salt and pepper

30 mL balsamic vinegar 2 tbsp

125 mL chopped fresh parsley 1/2 cup

Hot Pepper Oil

250 mL olive oil 1 cup

375 mL chopped red pepper 1 1/2 cups

3 cloves garlic, chopped 3

1/2 jalapeño pepper, chopped 1/2

2 mL ground annato or paprika 1/2 tsp

2 mL dried thyme 1/2 tsp

Pinch ground black pepper

1 bay leaf 1

METHOD

HOT PEPPER OIL

1 In a saucepan, heat 30 mL (2 tbsp) olive oil over high heat. Add the red pepper and cook until caramelized (3 minutes).

2 Add the garlic, jalapeño pepper and spices; cook for another minute. Reduce heat to low, pour in the remaining oil and simmer, uncovered, for 15 minutes.

3 Remove from heat, cool and filter through a strainer. Keep at room temperature.

PAN-FRIED SHRIMPS

1 In a large skillet, heat the pepper oil over high heat. Cook the shrimps for 2 to 3 minutes or until done. Remove from skillet and keep warm.

2 In the same skillet, sauté the green onion, and red and green pepper for 3 minutes over medium heat.

3 Add the beans, parsley, salt and pepper to taste, and continue cooking for 2 to 3 minutes or until the cooking liquid has evaporated. Deglaze with balsamic vinegar. Remove from heat.

4 Place the bean and pepper mixture on the plates, add the shrimps and pour over the remaining pepper oil.

Skate Wings with Sautéed Bean Sprouts

INGREDIENTS

1.5 kg cleaned skate wings, bone in 3 lb

4 to 6 servings

Marinade

125 mL chopped fresh lemon grass 1/2 cup

60 mL olive oil 1/4 cup

30 mL curry powder 2 tbsp

Juice of half a lemon

15 mL fish sauce 1 tbsp

15 mL sesame oil 1 tbsp

Sauté

15 mL olive oil 1 tbsp

60 g julienned red onion 1/4 cup

60 g julienned carrot 1/4 cup

60 g julienned red pepper 1/4 cup

1 can (375 mL/16-oz) baby corn, drained   1

500 g bean sprouts 1 lb

250 mL coarsely chopped watercress 1 cup

30 mL black bean and garlic sauce 2 tbsp

125 mL water or fish stock 1/2 cup

Salt and freshly ground pepper

60 mL chopped fresh coriander 1/4 cup
or 2 mL dried coriander 1/2 tsp

60 mL chopped green onion 1/4 cup

60 mL sesame seeds 1/4 cup

METHOD

MARINADE

In a large bowl, combine all the marinade ingredients and mix well. Add the skate and marinate for 1 hour in the refrigerator.

SAUTÉ

1   Heat a large nonstick skillet and cook the skate 3 to 4 minutes per side until the bone separates easily from the flesh. Remove from the skillet and keep warm.

2   In the same skillet, add the olive oil and sauté the julienned onion, carrot and red pepper for 2 to 3 minutes over medium heat.

3   Add the baby corn, bean sprouts, watercress and bean sauce. Continue cooking for 2 minutes.

4   Add water, season and heat thoroughly for 1 minute. Remove from heat.

5   Place the vegetable and bean sprout mixture on the plates, garnish with coriander, green onion and sesame seeds.

Chicken Supreme with Red Bean Compote

4 to 6 servings

INGREDIENTS

1 kg boneless chicken breasts 2 lb

Marinade

60 mL olive oil 1/4 cup

10 mL dried tarragon 2 tsp

5 mL paprika 1 tsp

2 mL dried thyme 1/2 tsp

Salt and freshly ground pepper

1 kg boneless chicken breasts 2 lb

Cream of Smoked Bacon

250 g smoked bacon, cut into strips 1/2 lb

250 g chopped onion 1 cup

2 cloves garlic, chopped 2

2 mL dried thyme 1/2 tsp

1 bay leaf 1

60 mL soy sauce 1/4 cup

1 L 35% cream 4 cups

Freshly ground pepper

Red Bean Compote

30 mL olive oil 2 tbsp

200 g red peppers, diced 7 oz

150 g orange peppers, cubed 5 1/2 oz

150 g yellow peppers, diced 5 1/2 oz

30 mL chopped green onion 2 tbsp

400 g cooked red beans or one 540 mL (19-oz) can red beans, rinsed and drained 2 cups

125 mL cream of smoked bacon 1/2 cup

Salt and pepper

60 g chopped fresh parsley 1/4 cup

METHOD

MARINADE

In a large bowl, mix the olive oil and spices. Add the chicken breasts and marinate for 1 hour in the refrigerator.

CREAM OF SMOKED BACON

1 In a large pot, cook the bacon strips over high heat for 3 minutes.

2 Discard the excess fat from the bacon leaving about 15 mL (1 tbsp) in the pot. Continue cooking over medium heat for 3 to 5 minutes until the bacon strips turn golden.

3 Add the onion, garlic, thyme and bay leaf. Cook for 2 more minutes.

4 Pour in the soy sauce, followed by the 35% cream. Add pepper and bring to a boil, uncovered, over low heat. Reduce the liquid by half. Remove from heat.

5 In a food processor or blender, purée until smooth (2 to 3 minutes). Strain. Keep warm.

RED BEAN COMPOTE

1 In a large skillet, heat the olive oil over medium heat and cook chicken breasts for 5 minutes per side or until the chicken is no longer pink. Remove from the skillet and keep warm.

2 In the same skillet, add the peppers and green onion. Cook for 3 minutes.

3 Add the red beans and cook for another 2 minutes. Pour in 60 mL (1/4 cup) cream of smoked bacon.

4 Season, bring to a boil and remove from heat. Sprinkle with parsley.

5 Place the beans and peppers on the plates, add the chicken breasts and pour over the remaining cream of smoked bacon.

Grilled Pork Chops with Green Split Pea Purée

INGREDIENTS

60 mL olive oil **1/4 cup**
15 mL Worcestershire sauce **1 tbsp**
10 mL dried oregano **2 tsp**
5 mL paprika **1 tsp**
Salt and freshly ground pepper
1 kg pork chops **2 lb**

Green Split Pea Purée

15 mL olive oil **1 tbsp**
1 clove garlic, chopped **1**
30 mL chopped green onion **2 tbsp**
800 g cooked green split peas **4 cups**
125 mL 35% cream **1/2 cup**
Salt and pepper
60 g butter, cubed **2 oz**

Mustard Sauce

15 mL olive oil **1 tbsp**
15 mL chopped green onion **1 tbsp**
125 mL 35% cream **1/2 cup**
500 mL water or chicken stock **2 cups**
Salt and pepper
15 mL cornstarch **1 tbsp**
45 mL water **3 tbsp**
30 mL mustard seeds **2 tbsp**
2 mL Dijon mustard **1/2 tsp**

METHOD

4 to 6 servings

MARINADE

In a large bowl, blend the oil, Worcestershire sauce and spices. Place the pork chops in the marinade and refrigerate for 1 hour in the refrigerator.

GREEN SPLIT PEA PURÉE

1 In a 2 L (8-cup) pot, heat the olive oil over medium heat; cook garlic and green onion for 2 minutes.

2 Add the green peas and 35% cream. Season and boil, uncovered, for 2 minutes. Remove from heat.

3 Purée in a food processor and pass through a strainer. Add the butter gradually, blending gently. Keep warm.

MUSTARD SAUCE

1 In a 2 L (8-cup) pot, heat the olive oil over medium heat and cook the green onions for 2 minutes.

2 Pour in the cream and stock. Bring to a boil, season, lower the heat and simmer, uncovered, for 2 minutes.

3 In a small bowl, mix the cornstarch with 45 mL (3 tbsp) cold water.

4 Pour the cornstarch into the mixture in a stream, whisking constantly, over low heat. Boil for 1 minute, stirring constantly. Remove from heat.

5 Add both mustards, whisking vigorously. Keep warm.

GRILLED PORK CHOPS

1 Preheat the barbecue or the oven broiler to medium heat. Place the pork chops on the barbecue grill or broiling pan. Cook for 4 to 5 minutes per side until the meat is no longer pink inside.

2 Arrange the pork chops on the plates next to the purée and top with mustard sauce.

Veal Medallions with Small Red Beans and Duxelles

4 to 6 servings

INGREDIENTS

1 kg larded veal medallions, in fillets about 2.5 cm (1 inch) thick and 6 to 7 cm (2 1/2 inches) in diameter **2 lb**

Marinade

60 mL olive oil **1/4 cup**

30 mL dried tarragon **2 tbsp**

5 mL paprika **1 tsp**

15 mL Worcestershire sauce **1 tbsp**

Salt and pepper

Small Red Beans

15 mL olive oil **1 tbsp**

125 mL chopped green onion **1/2 cup**

2 cloves garlic **2**

400 g cooked small red beans or one 540 mL (19-oz) can red beans, rinsed and drained **2 cups**

Duxelles

250 mL 35% cream **1 cup**

Salt and pepper

60 mL fresh parsley **1/4 cup**

Duxelles

350 g mushrooms, cleaned **12 oz**

2 green onions **2**

10 mL butter **2 tsp**

Salt and pepper

METHOD

MARINADE

In a large bowl, mix all the marinade ingredients. Place the veal medallions in the marinade and refrigerate for at least 1 hour.

DUXELLES

1 In a food processor, finely chop the mushrooms and green onions.

2 In a skillet, heat the butter over medium heat and add the chopped mushroom mixture. Season with salt and pepper. Cook over low heat, uncovered, for about 10 minutes or until cooking liquid has evaporated. Set aside.

MEDALLIONS

1 In a nonstick skillet, cook the medallions for 2 minutes per side or until the meat is no longer pink in the middle. Remove from heat and keep warm.

2 In the same skillet, heat the olive oil. Sauté the green onion, garlic and red beans for 3 minutes. Add the duxelles and cream.

3 Season and bring to a boil. Boil for 2 minutes or until the cream has thickened. Remove from heat and sprinkle with parsley.

4 Serve the veal medallions with the bean and duxelle mixture.

Braised Rabbit with Black Beans

4 to 6 servings

INGREDIENTS

60 mL olive oil **1/4 cup**

2 kg rabbit, cut into large pieces **4 lb**

250 mL chopped onion **1 cup**

250 g chopped carrot **5 1/2 oz**

250 g chopped celery **5 1/2 oz**

2 cloves garlic, chopped **2**

500 mL chicken stock or water **2 cups**

Salt and pepper

800 g cooked black beans or two 540 mL (19-oz) cans black beans, rinsed and drained **4 cups**

Marinade

250 mL dry white wine **1 cup**

5 mL ground fennel seeds **1 tsp**

5 mL crushed coriander seeds **1 tsp**

5 mL ground anise seeds **1 tsp**

5 mL ground cardamom seeds **1 tsp**

5 mL ground caraway seeds **1 tsp**

METHOD

MARINADE

In a large bowl, mix all the marinade ingredients. Place the rabbit pieces in the marinade and refrigerate for at least 6 hours.

BRAISED RABBIT

1 Preheat the oven to 220°C (425°F).

2 In a large skillet, heat the olive oil over high heat and sear the meat 3 minutes per side. Remove the meat and place in a large ovenproof casserole dish.

3 Add the vegetables and garlic to the casserole dish. Pour in the chicken stock and add salt and pepper. Cover and bake in the oven for 1 hour at 220°C (425°F).

4 Uncover the dish and lower the oven temperature to 180°C (350°F). Bake for another 30 minutes. Baste the rabbit pieces with cooking juices every 15 minutes. Remove the dish from the oven, remove the meat and keep warm.

5 Pour the vegetables and cooking liquid into a 4 L (16-cup) casserole dish, defat the liquid and add the black beans. Simmer over low heat, half-covered, for 30 minutes.

6 Pour the bean and vegetable mixture into deep plates, and place the rabbit meat around it; drizzle with the cooking juices.

Quail Duo on a Bed of Lentils

4 to 6 servings

INGREDIENTS

1.5 kg quail, deboned **3 lb**

30 mL olive oil **2 tbsp**

500 g red onions, sliced **1 lb**

2 kg kale, sliced **2 lb**

500 g red apples, peeled and diced **1 lb**

400 mL small brown lentils, cooked, or one 540 mL (19-oz) can brown lentils, rinsed and drained **2 cups**

125 mL cider vinegar **1/2 cup**

Salt and pepper

60 mL fresh parsley, chopped **1/4 cup**

Marinade

60 mL olive oil **1/4 cup**

5 mL dried basil **1 tsp**

2 mL dried thyme **1/2 tsp**

15 mL Worcestershire sauce **1 tbsp**

30 mL Calvados **2 tbsp**

Pinch cayenne pepper

Salt and pepper

METHOD

MARINADE

In a large bowl, mix all the marinade ingredients. Place the quail in the marinade and refrigerate for at least 2 hours.

QUAIL DUO

1 In a large nonstick skillet, fry the quail over high heat for 3 minutes per side or until the meat is no longer pink on the inside. Remove from heat and keep warm.

2 To the same skillet, add the olive oil and cook the onions for 2 to 3 minutes over medium heat. Add the kale and cook for 5 minutes. Add the apples and lentils, and cook for another 3 minutes over high heat.

3 Deglaze with 60 mL (1/4 cup) cider vinegar, season with salt and pepper and cook for another 2 minutes. Remove from heat and sprinkle with parsley.

4 Serve the lentil and cabbage mixture in the middle of the plates, with the quail arranged on top and drizzled with the remaining cider vinegar.

Turkey Paupiettes with Lima Beans

4 to 6 servings

INGREDIENTS

180 mL sliced carrots **3/4 cup**
180 mL sliced zucchini **3/4 cup**
180 mL sliced daikon* **3/4 cup**
1 kg flattened turkey cutlets **2 lb**
24 toothpicks **24**

Marinade

60 mL soy sauce **1/4 cup**
30 mL honey **2 tbsp**
60 mL vegetable oil **1/4 cup**
60 mL hoisin sauce **1/4 cup**
30 mL sesame oil **2 tbsp**

Lima Beans with Nectarines

15 mL olive oil **1 tbsp**
500 g pitted nectarines **1 lb**
2 mL brown sugar **1/2 tsp**
60 mL chopped green onion **1/4 cup**
1 clove garlic, chopped **1**
400 g cooked lima beans or one 540 mL (19-oz) can lima beans, rinsed and drained **2 cups**
Salt and pepper
Juice of half a lime
125 mL chicken stock or water **1/2 cup**
60 g diced butter **2 oz**
60 mL chopped fresh coriander **1/4 cup**
or **2 mL** dried coriander **1/2 tsp**

METHOD

MARINADE

In a large bowl, whisk together all the liquid ingredients. Add the turkey cutlets and marinate for 6 hours in the refrigerator.

PAUPIETTES

1 In a salad bowl, mix the carrots, zucchini and daikon. Set aside at room temperature.

2 Remove the meat from the marinade, drain well and lay flat on a work surface.

3 Portion out the vegetable mixture in the middle of the cutlets, roll and fasten with 2 toothpicks. Refrigerate.

LIMA BEANS WITH NECTARINES

1 In a large, very hot nonstick skillet, cook the paupiettes for 4 to 5 minutes or until the meat is no longer pink in the centre. Remove from heat and keep warm.

2 To the same pan, heat the olive oil over high heat and add the nectarines and sugar; cook for 2 minutes until golden. Transfer to another container and keep warm.

3 In the same pan, sauté the green onion and garlic for 1 minute. Add the beans, season and continue cooking for 2 to 3 more minutes over high heat. Deglaze with the lime juice, pour in the chicken stock and bring to a boil.

4 Remove from heat. Gradually add the butter, stirring gently. Sprinkle with chopped coriander.

*Daikon is also known as "Japanese radish."

Lamb Chops with Provençal-style Chickpeas

INGREDIENTS

1.5 kg lamb chops 3 lb

Marinade

30 mL olive oil 2 tbsp

1 clove garlic, chopped 1

15 mL Dijon mustard 1 tbsp

2 mL dried thyme 1/2 tsp

5 mL oregano 1 tsp

5 mL basil 1 tsp

10 mL paprika 2 tsp

Pinch ground white pepper

Pinch cayenne pepper

Salt and freshly ground pepper

Provençal-style Chickpeas

15 mL olive oil 1 tbsp

175 mL chopped onion 3/4 cup

100 g mushrooms, minced 3 1/2 oz

2 cloves garlic, chopped 2

400 g cooked chickpeas or one
540 mL (19-oz) can chickpeas,
rinsed and drained 2 cups

60 mL pastis 1/4 cup

250 mL fresh tomatoes, seeded and
chopped 1 cup

60 mL parsley 1/4 cup

M ETHOD

MARINADE

In a large bowl, blend all the ingredients of the marinade, add the lamb chops and marinate for 1 hour in the refrigerator.

PROVENÇAL-STYLE CHICKPEAS

1 In a large nonstick skillet, sear the chops for 3 minutes per side, or according to preference. Remove from heat and keep warm.

2 To the same pan, add the olive oil and, over medium heat, sauté the onion for 3 to 5 minutes until caramelized.

3 Add the mushrooms and garlic; cook for 2 minutes. Add the chickpeas and the tomatoes and cook for another 2 minutes over high heat.

4 Deglaze with the pastis and cook for 2 minutes. Remove from heat and sprinkle with parsley.

5 Arrange the chickpea mixture on the plates and place the chops on top.

Any other anise-flavoured liqueur can be substituted for the pastis.

Tournedos with Mixed Beans Ratatouille

Tournedos with Mixed Beans Ratatouille

INGREDIENTS

4 to 6 servings

Mixed Bean Ratatouille

15 mL olive oil 1 tbsp

175 mL chopped onion 3/4 cup

1 clove garlic, chopped 1

15 mL tomato paste 1 tbsp

796 mL diced tomatoes 26 oz

400 g cooked mixed beans or one 540 mL (19-oz) can mixed beans, rinsed and drained 2 cups

1 mL dried thyme 1/4 tsp

2 mL dried oregano 1/2 tsp

2 mL dried basil 1/2 tsp

Pinch brown sugar

Salt and pepper

Tournedos

1 kg beef fillets (medallions) 2 lb

15 mL olive oil 1 tbsp

30 mL green onion, chopped 2 tbsp

1 mL dried thyme 1/4 tsp

2 mL dried oregano 1/2 tsp

Pinch freshly ground black pepper

250 mL dry red wine 1 cup

125 g butter, cubed 4 oz

Salt and pepper

METHOD

MIXED BEAN RATATOUILLE

1 In a 2 L (8-cup) saucepan, heat the olive oil and cook the onion, garlic and tomato paste over low heat for 3 minutes.

2 Add the tomatoes and their juice, beans, spices, sugar, salt and pepper, and simmer over low heat, uncovered, for 15 minutes or until the tomato liquid has been slightly reduced. Remove from heat and keep warm.

TOURNEDOS

1 In a large nonstick skillet, cook the tournedos for 2 to 3 minutes per side over high heat or according to preference. Transfer to another container and keep warm.

2 To the same skillet, add the olive oil and cook the green onion with the spices for 2 minutes. Deglaze the skillet with red wine, bring to a boil and reduce by half over high heat.

3 Remove from heat and gradually whisk in the butter cubes. Adjust the seasoning and keep warm.

4 Serve the ratatouille with the tournedos on top and drizzle with the red wine sauce.

Veal Kidneys with Black-eyed Peas

INGREDIENTS

1 kg veal kidneys, fat removed and cut into 2.5 cm (1-inch) cubes **2 lb**

4 to 6 servings

Marinade

60 mL olive oil **1/4 cup**

15 mL Dijon mustard **1 tbsp**

5 mL oregano **1 tsp**

2 mL thyme **1/2 tsp**

5 mL chili powder **1 tsp**

Freshly ground pepper

8 to 12 wooden skewers **8 to 12**

Cumin-flavoured Black-eyed Peas

15 mL olive oil **1 tbsp**

180 mL chopped onion **3/4 cup**

125 mL chopped carrot **1/2 cup**

125 mL chopped mushrooms **1/2 cup**

125 mL chopped red pepper **1/2 cup**

2 cloves garlic, chopped **2**

2 mL cumin seeds **1/2 tsp**

400 g cooked black-eyed peas or one 540 mL (19-oz) can black-eyed peas, rinsed and drained **2 cups**

250 mL 35% cream **1 cup**

Pinch cayenne pepper

Salt and pepper

60 mL chopped fresh parsley **1/4 cup**

METHOD

MARINADE

In a bowl, blend all the ingredients. Add the kidney cubes. Marinate for 4 to 6 hours in the refrigerator. Thread the kidney pieces onto the skewers and refrigerate.

BLACK-EYED PEAS

1 In a 2 L (8-cup) saucepan, heat the olive oil over high heat and sauté the onion, carrot, mushrooms, pepper, garlic and cumin for 3 minutes until caramelized.

2 Add the peas and cook for another 2 minutes. Pour in the cream, season and bring to a boil. Lower heat to minimum and simmer, uncovered, for 2 to 3 minutes.

3 Remove from heat and sprinkle with parsley. Keep warm.

4 Preheat the barbecue or the oven broiler to medium. Place the brochettes on the barbecue grill or broiler pan. Grill for about 5 minutes, turning regularly.

5 Serve the brochettes with the black-eyed peas and, if desired, home-made french fries.

Magrets of Duck with Kiwis and Snow Peas

4 to 6 servings

INGRÉDIENTS

1 kg duck cutlets 2 lb

Marinade

60 mL honey 1/4 cup

60 mL soy sauce 1/4 cup

250 mL orange juice 1 cup

15 mL chopped ginger 1 tbsp

1 clove garlic, chopped 1

Kiwis and Snow Peas

30 mL chopped green onion 2 tbsp

125 mL sliced red pepper 1/2 cup

175 mL sliced carrot 3/4 cup

500 g snow peas, cleaned, blanched but still crisp 1 lb

1 can baby corn (450 mL/6-oz), drained 1

10 mL brown sugar 2 tsp

30 mL rice vinegar 2 tbsp

175 mL chicken stock or water 3/4 cup

30 mL butter 2 tbsp

Salt and pepper

4 kiwis, peeled and puréed 4

METHOD

MARINADE

In a large bowl, whisk together all ingredients. Add the duck and marinate for 6 hours in the refrigerator.

KIWIS AND SNOW PEAS

1 Preheat the oven to 240°C (475°F).

2 Heat a nonstick skillet over high heat. Place the cutlets skin side down and cook for 3 minutes. Turn and cook for another 2 to 3 minutes.

3 Remove the cutlets and place in an oven-proof dish, skin side up. Bake the cutlets for 5 minutes in a 240°C (475°F) oven. Remove from heat and keep warm.

4 Discard the excess cooking fat, saving about 15 mL (1 tbsp). Add green onion, pepper and carrot and cook over high heat for 2 minutes.

5 Add the snow peas, baby corn and sugar, and cook for 2 to 3 more minutes. Deglaze with rice vinegar. Remove the vegetables from the skillet and keep warm.

6 Add the stock to the skillet, bring to a boil, add salt and pepper, and reduce the heat. Gradually whisk in the butter and the kiwi.

7 Thinly slice the cutlets and place on the plates. Serve with the snow pea mixture and top with kiwi sauce.

Leg of Wild Boar with Mousseline of Yellow Split Peas

4 to 6 servings

INGREDIENTS

Marinade

1 clove garlic, chopped **1**

5 mL paprika **1 tsp**

2 mL dried thyme **1/2 tsp**

5 mL dried tarragon **1 tsp**

500 mL dry red wine **2 cups**

Leg of Wild Boar

1 kg leg of wild boar, boned and fat removed, cut into 2.5 cm (1-inch) pieces **2 lb**

60 mL brown sugar **1/4 cup**

250 g fresh cranberries, washed **1/2 lb**

30 mL balsamic vinegar **2 tbsp**

500 mL water **2 cups**

60 g butter, cubed **2 oz**

Mousseline

15 mL olive oil **1 tbsp**

1 clove garlic **1**

30 mL chopped green onions **2 tbsp**

800 g yellow split peas, cooked **4 cups**

150 mL 35% cream **2/3 cup**

Salt and pepper

60 g butter, cubed **2 oz**

METHOD

MARINADE

In a medium-sized bowl, mix the garlic, spices and 250 mL (1 cup) red wine. Add the boar cubes and marinate for 12 hours in the refrigerator.

LEG OF WILD BOAR

1 Pour the red wine and sugar into a 2 L (8-cup) saucepan. Boil over high heat, uncovered, for 2 minutes. Add the cranberries and lower the heat to minimum; cook for 5 minutes. Cranberries should still be crunchy. Remove the cranberries and set aside.

2 Over high heat, reduce the syrup, uncovered, for 3 to 5 minutes or until it begins to caramelize. Stop the caramelization by adding vinegar and water. Bring to a boil, uncovered, and reduce by half and remove from heat.

3 Gradually whisk in the butter and add the cranberries. Keep warm.

4 Remove the boar cubes from the marinade and drain well.

5 In a very hot, nonstick pan, cook the boar for about 5 minutes or to desired degree of doneness. Season with salt and pepper. Remove from heat and keep warm.

MOUSSELINE

1 In a 2 L (8-cup) saucepan, heat the oil over medium heat and cook the garlic and green onions for 2 minutes.

2 Add the yellow split peas and cream. Season and cook, uncovered, for 2 minutes. Remove from heat.

3 Using a food processor, purée and pass through a strainer. Add the butter little by little, stirring gently. Keep warm.

4 Pile the mousseline in the middle of the plates and arrange the boar cubes around the edge. Cover with cranberry sauce.

Loin of Deer with Flageolets

Pheasant or moose can be substituted for the deer.

4 to 6 servings

Loin of Deer with Flageolets

INGREDIENTS

1 kg loin of venison, boned and fat removed **2 lb**

Marinade

30 mL olive oil **2 tbsp**

1 mL dried thyme **1/4 tsp**

5 mL dried oregano **1 tsp**

5 mL paprika **1 tsp**

Pinch cayenne pepper

Freshly ground pepper

2 cloves garlic, chopped **2**

Filbert Sauce

125 g butter, cut into large cubes **4 oz**

175 mL water **3/4 cup**

150 g toasted filberts **1/2 cup**

Salt and pepper

Flageolets and Leeks

15 mL olive oil **1 tbsp**

175 mL chopped carrots **3/4 cup**

175 mL chopped red pepper **3/4 cup**

2 leeks, white part only, washed and finely chopped **2**

1 clove garlic, chopped **1**

Pinch dried thyme

2 mL dried oregano **1/2 tsp**

400 g cooked flageolets or one 540 mL (19-oz) can flageolets, rinsed and drained **2 cups**

Salt and pepper

METHOD

MARINADE

In a medium-sized bowl, blend the oil, spices and garlic. Cut the loin of venison in 4 to 6 pieces of about 4 by 10 cm (2 by 4 inches) and place in a bowl. Allow to marinate for 6 hours in the refrigerator.

LOIN OF DEER

1   In a medium-sized skillet, heat the olive oil over high heat and cook the carrots and pepper for 3 minutes.

2   Add the leeks, garlic and spices. Reduce heat to medium and cook for 5 more minutes. Add the flageolets, salt and pepper and cook for 2 to 3 more minutes. Remove from heat and keep warm.

3   Preheat the oven to 220°C (425°F).

4   In a very hot nonstick skillet, cook the venison for 5 to 8 minutes or to desired degree of doneness. Remove the meat from the pan and leave at room temperature for about 10 minutes.

5   In the same pan, melt the butter over medium heat and cook until it is a golden colour. Stop the butter from cooking by gradually adding water. Add the filberts, season and heat for 2 minutes without boiling. Remove from heat and keep warm.

6   Cut the meat into thin slices and place in an ovenproof dish. Reheat in the oven at 220°C (425°F) for 2 to 3 minutes.

7   Remove from the oven and place on plates. Serve with the flageolet and leek mixture, and the filbert sauce.

Side Dishes

Side Dishes

Mixed Bean Curry

Two-Colour Split Pea Purée

Mung Bean and Basmati Rice Croquettes

Small Lima Beans à la Française

Gratin of Flageolets and Leeks

Caribbean-style Black-eyed Peas

Mixed Bean Curry

6 to 8 servings

INGREDIENTS

15 mL olive oil 1 tbsp

125 mL chopped green onions 1/2 cup

2 cloves garlic, chopped 2

800 g cooked mixed beans, or two 540 mL (19-oz) cans mixed beans, rinsed and drained 4 cups

10 mL curry powder 2 tsp

125 mL coconut milk 1/2 cup

125 mL 35% cream 1/2 cup

Salt and pepper

Pinch cayenne pepper

125 mL chopped fresh coriander 1/2 cup

METHOD

1 In a medium-sized saucepan, heat olive oil and sauté the green onions and garlic for 2 minutes over high heat.

2 Add the beans and curry powder and cook for 2 minutes. Pour in the coconut milk and 35% cream. Season with salt, pepper and cayenne pepper. Bring to a boil and reduce heat.

3 Simmer for about 10 minutes, uncovered, or until sauce has thickened.

4 Remove from heat and add chopped coriander. Serve very hot.

Serve with pan-fried fish, leg of lamb or cutlets.

Two-Colour Split Pea Purée

6 to 8 servings

INGREDIENTS

30 mL olive oil 2 tbsp

30 mL chopped green onion 2 tbsp

500 g cooked green split peas 2 cups

125 mL 35% cream 1/4 cup

Salt and pepper

60 g butter, diced 2 oz

500 g cooked yellow split peas 2 cups

METHOD

1 Purée the green and yellow peas separately.

2 In a medium pot, cook 15 mL (1 tbsp) green onions for 2 minutes in 15 mL (1 tbsp) olive oil over low heat.

3 Add the cooked green split peas and 60 mL (1/4 cup) 35% cream. Boil, uncovered, for 2 minutes. Remove from heat.

4 Purée in a food processor and then strain. Gradually add 30 g (1 oz) butter, stirring gently. Keep warm.

5 Repeat the same procedure for the yellow split peas.

6 To serve, use a 10 cm by 5 cm (4- by 2-inch) circular form to divide the two purées equally within the circle.

This dish complements pork, poultry and venison.

Mung Bean and Basmati Rice Croquettes

6 to 8 servings

INDIA

The croquette mixture may be prepared a few hours in advance and refrigerated.

INGREDIENTS

15 mL olive oil **1 tbsp**

30 mL green onions, chopped **2 tbsp**

500 g mung beans **2 cups**

5 mL garam masala or Chinese five-spice powder **1 tsp**

Salt and pepper

500 mL cooked basmati rice **2 cups**

80 mL grated Parmesan **1/3 mL**

60 mL chopped fresh parsley **1/4 cup**

2 eggs, beaten **2**

METHOD

1 In a medium-sized skillet, heat the olive oil over high heat and cook the green onions for 2 minutes.

2 Add the mung beans and garam masala. Season and cook for 3 minutes over medium heat. Reduce the heat and let cool completely.

3 In a large bowl, mix the beans, cooked rice, Parmesan, parsley and beaten eggs. Shape the mixture into 7.5 cm (3-inch) croquettes. Refrigerate.

4 Just before serving, heat the croquettes in a nonstick pan over medium heat for 2 to 3 minutes per side.

Small Lima Beans à la Française

4 to 6 servings

FRANCE

INGREDIENTS

15 ml butter **1 tbsp**

250 g pearl onions **1/2 lb**

2 mL dried thyme **1/2 tsp**

Pinch brown sugar

Salt and pepper

400 g cooked small lima beans or one 540 mL (19-oz) can lima beans, rinsed and drained **2 cups**

125 mL 35% cream **1/2 cup**

1 head romaine lettuce, washed and shredded **1**

2 mL Dijon mustard **1/2 tsp**

METHOD

1 Melt the butter in a 2 L (8-cup) saucepan over medium heat.

2 Add the pearl onions, thyme, salt, pepper and sugar and cook over high heat for 3 to 5 minutes or until the mixture is caramelized.

3 Add the beans and heat for 2 more minutes over medium heat.

   Deglaze with the cream and bring to a boil for 2 minutes, uncovered, to reduce it slightly.

4 Add the lettuce and mustard to the saucepan and mix well. Reheat the bean and lettuce mixture over medium heat for 2 minutes.Serve hot.

Gratin of Flageolets and Leeks

4 to 6 servings

INGREDIENTS

15 mL olive oil **1 tbsp**

3 leeks, white part only, washed and minced **3**

2 cloves garlic, chopped **2**

1 mL thyme **1/4 tsp**

2 mL tarragon **1/2 tsp**

Salt and pepper

400 g cooked flageolets or one 540 mL (19-oz) can flageolets, rinsed and drained **2 cups**

125 mL breadcrumbs **1/2 cup**

125 mL melted butter **1/2 cup**

Salt and pepper

M ETHOD

1 In a medium-sized skillet, heat the olive oil over medium heat and cook the leeks for 5 minutes. Add the garlic, spices and flageolets.

2 Cook over high heat for 2 minutes.

3 Transfer the mixture to an ovenproof dish. Cover with the breadcrumbs and melted butter.

4 Broil for 3 to 5 minutes or until the breadcrumbs are a golden colour. Serve hot.

Caribbean-style Black-eyed Peas

4 to 6 servings

Ideal to serve with Creole dishes.

INGREDIENTS

30 mL olive oil **2 tbsp**

175 mL chopped green pepper **3/4 cup**

175 mL chopped red pepper **3/4 cup**

150 mL chopped green onions **1/2 cup**

2 mL chopped fresh ginger **1/2 tsp**

2 cloves garlic, chopped **2**

2 mL dried thyme **1/2 tsp**

1 mL ground nutmeg **1/4 tsp**

2 mL ground allspice **1/2 tsp**

1 mL ground cinnamon **1/4 tsp**

Pinch cayenne pepper

400 g cooked black-eyed peas or one 540 mL (19-oz) can black-eyed peas, rinsed and drained **2 cups**

Salt and pepper

Juice of 1 lime

60 mL fresh parsley, chopped **1/4 cup**

M ETHOD

1 In a large skillet, heat all the ingredients except the peas for 5 minutes over medium heat. Add the peas, season and cook for another 2 to 3 minutes.

2 Remove from heat, add the lime juice and sprinkle with parsley. Serve hot or cold.

Index